Ee Ff Gg Hh Ii

Nn Oo Pp Qq

Ww Xx Yy Zz

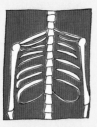

A catalogue record for this book is available from the British Library

Published by Ladybird Books Ltd
80 Strand London WC2R 0RL
A Penguin Company

008
© LADYBIRD BOOKS LTD MMIX
LADYBIRD and the device of a Ladybird are trademarks of Ladybird Books Ltd

ISBN-13: 978 1 40930 221 6

Printed in China

Picture
Dictionary

illustrated by Mark Chambers

Aa

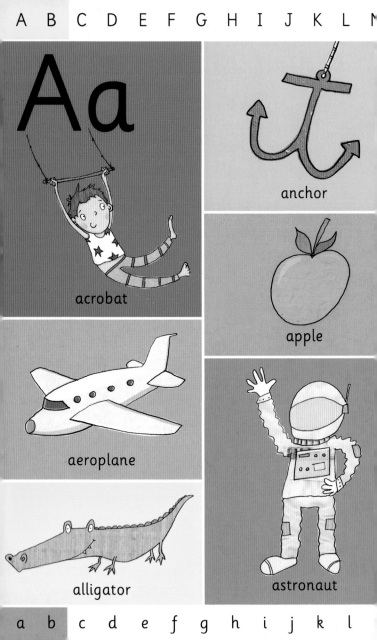

acrobat

anchor

apple

aeroplane

alligator

astronaut

Bb

ball

bird

banana

butterfly

basket

buttons

Cc

car

chair

castle

clock

cat

clown

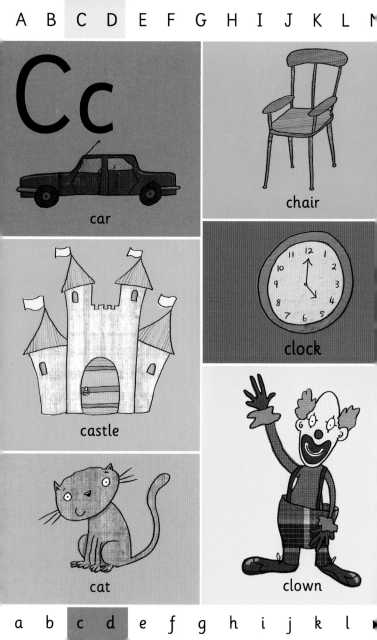

Dd

digger

doll

dinosaur

drum

dog

duck

Ee

eagle

elephant

envelope

earrings

egg

explorer

Ff

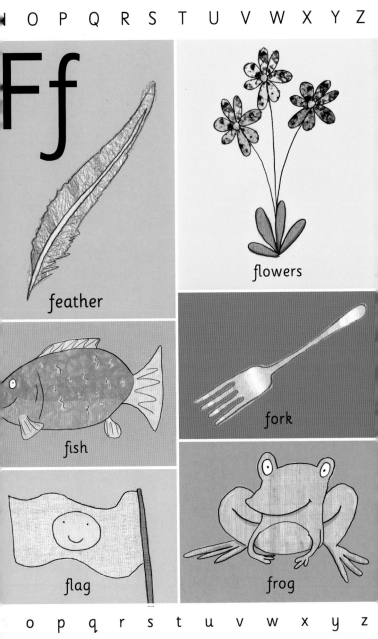

feather

flowers

fish

fork

flag

frog

Gg

garage

glass

gate

goat

ghost

guitar

Hh

helicopter

hammer

horse

hands

hat

house

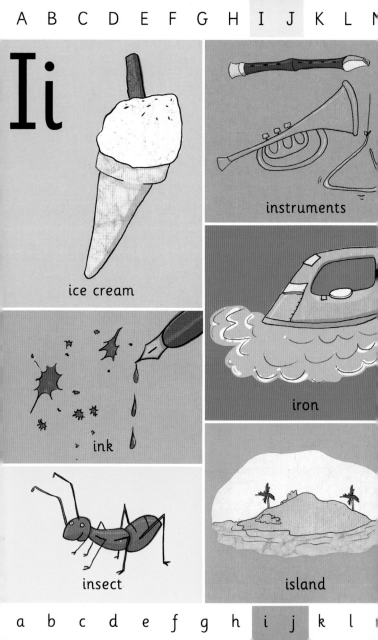

Ii

ice cream

instruments

ink

iron

insect

island

Jj

jacket

jam

jigsaw

jug

juggler

jungle

Kk

kangaroo

keys

king

knife

knitting

koala

Ll

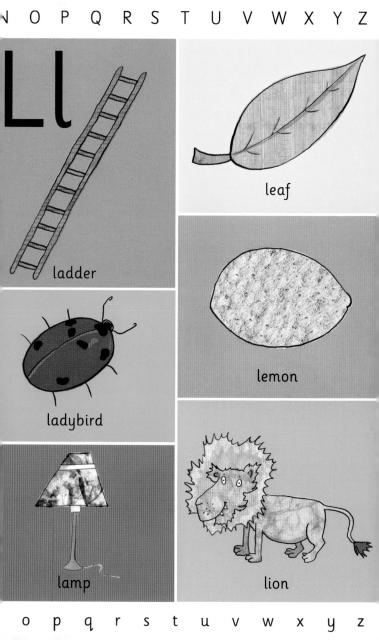

ladder

leaf

ladybird

lemon

lamp

lion

Mm

map

moon

mirror

mountain

monkey

mouse

Nn

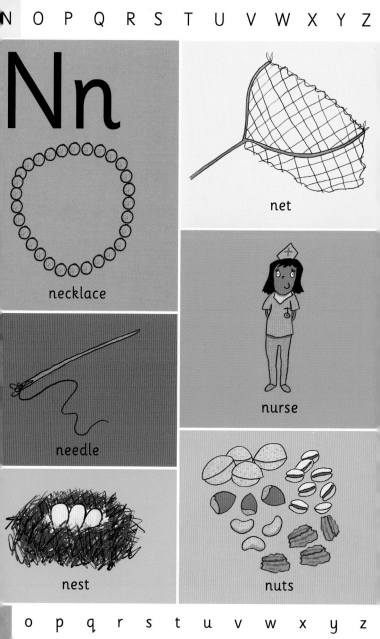

necklace

net

needle

nurse

nest

nuts

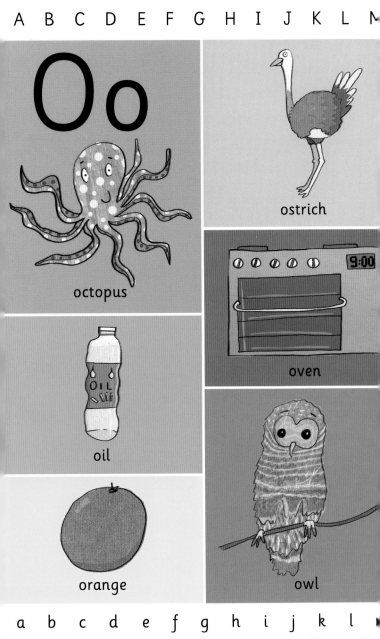

Oo

octopus

ostrich

oil

oven

orange

owl

Pp

paint

penguin

palace

piano

pencil

pie

Qq

quarter

quiet

queen

quick

question

quilt

Rr

rabbit

robot

radio

rose

rainbow

ruler

Ss

sheep

shoes

snake

spider

star

sun

Tt

table

tools

telephone

tree

tiger

trumpet

Uu

umbrella

unicorn

underground

uniform

underwear

universe

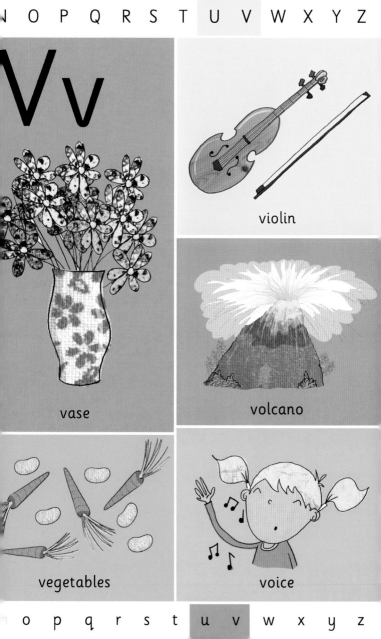

Vv

vase

violin

volcano

vegetables

voice

Ww

waterfall

windmill

web

whale

whistle

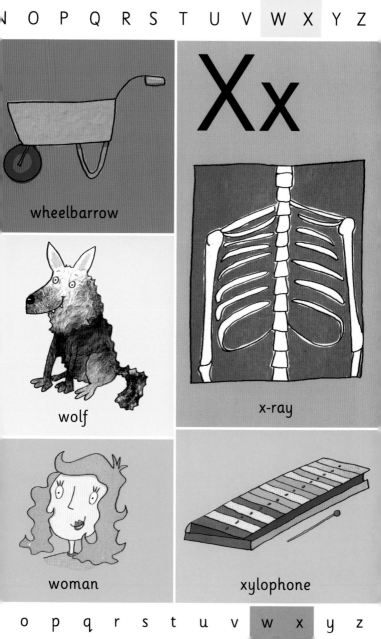

wheelbarrow

Xx

wolf

x-ray

woman

xylophone

Yy

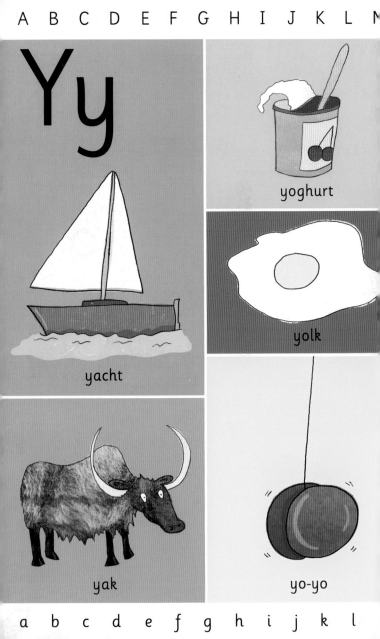

yoghurt

yolk

yacht

yak

yo-yo